Of Darkness and Light

A dark poetry collection

Despoina Kemeridou

Cover Illustration: Evangelos Dimou
www.iamevandimu.com
Editing-Correction: Despoina Kemeridou, Evangelos Dimou
Pagination: Evangelos Dimou

**© 2021 SELF-PUBLISHING "KEMERIDOU"
DESPOINA KEMERIDOU**
website: www.kemeridou.com
email: books@kemeridou.com

Of Darkness and Light

A dark poetry collection

www.kemeridou.com

2020

Introduction

Dear reader,

This is going to be short, so please bear with me and take the time to read it.

As the subtitle suggests, this is a collection of **dark** poems. There are mentions of sensitive topics (suicide, death etc.), so it's better to stop here, if you think you can't continue.

I would like to make clear, that none of these poems express how I am feeling or indicate my state of mind. Maybe it is the darkness of my past, still haunting me to this day. However, there is always a way out of darkness; the road to light, the one I chose to follow.

Should you feel any type of negative emotion, I will always be available to hear you out. Don't hesitate to contact me on any of my social media accounts or per email.

Love,
Despoina Kemeridou

To darkness, whom I'll always visit.
To light, who will always save me.

*"For light exists only with darkness,
and darkness can't be without light."*

Come with me.
Follow me into the darkness,
as I lead you
to the place you longed to be.

Be one with me.
Join this dance.
Be one with darkness.
Eternally.

For light exists only with darkness,
and darkness can't be without light.
For our world was born in darkness,
and that is what we'll forever be.

Her Darkness

Nobody asked how she felt.

Nobody cared.

Ignored forever.

And the pain grew bigger,

until she couldn't take it anymore.

If only she could be understood.

Was she asking for too much?

Every day, a darkness.

Every darkness, ever darkening.

Sinking...

Deeper and deeper into despair.

Until it consumed her.

Alone.

Always alone.

Suffocating Pain

What if my life

is just a thread,

which I can cut

with scissors in hand,

just to break free

from this wasteland?

And if this is true,

then surely, I will.

I'll open my wings

with another pill.

Childhood, Gone

A lifeless unicorn,

cruelly murdered.

A child's hopes,

grains in the sand.

Dreams long forgotten.

Memories gone.

End of the road.

Home, no more.

Burial

Burry me deep.

Forget about me.

Erase our memories.

Carry the pain.

For I won't be there.

Alone you'll stay.

After my death,

no one will smile.

What happiness?

Devastation is yours.

Death of Love

I lie motionless.

I do not breathe.

He used his hooks.

He drew me in.

A lifeless body.

A voiceless scream.

Just let me die.

Just set me free.

Bittersweet Ending

Like a script from a tragedy,

my life's ending.

Like a fish on land,

my breathing, slow.

Like the sun that will never rise again,

the memory of me will fade.

Gone.

Forgotten.

Alone.

Soul in the Water

Oh, how I long to follow you
somewhere in the deepest ocean,
lost among the waves.
There, my sorrow I'll drown.

My lungs will fill with water.
So I'll no longer scream your name.
And as I'm dying,
my eyes will remain open,
looking up to the night sky.

Moon and stars,
together we will die.

Dead or Alive

The world is moving,

but I'm still here.

Frozen in place,

I can't break free.

What does life mean,

if you can't live?

Maybe it's death,

since I can't be.

Who was I?

I have forgotten.

And all my words,

they are now rotten.

Oath of Love

All for your love,

I can endure.

Pain, despair,

bring it my way.

But this, my love,

this, I can't.

The oath I gave you,

I must break.

For I can't do this.

I cannot live,

if you, my love,

are not with me.

Just give me poison,
a deadly dose.
So I can meet you
in a life unknown.

Deep Inside

Sinking, sinking,

deeper in these waters.

Feeling, hurting,

all is the same.

Screaming, screaming,

louder than my pain.

Falling to my knees,

I break, I break.

Crying, crying,

For all that I've lost.

Nothing is the same

nor will it ever be.

Emptiness, nothingness,

what I have left.

Darkness, lifeless,

what I will be.

Pain of Separation

What happiness should I speak of,

when you're so far away?

Away from my heart.

Away from my pain.

What is a dream worth,

if I can't share it with you?

With you, my only love.

With you, my only death.

Game Over

All is gone now.

All is over.

Always away.

Never forgotten.

Tried so hard,

but it's game over.

Winners none,

but losers many.

Broken pieces

and hearts, empty.

Silent Scream

I try to scream,

but no one listens.

Deep in my heart,

a child, hurt.

If they could hear

my deepest fear.

The silence,

it kills me.

Again, and again,

until I'm empty.

An empty shell,

with feelings plenty.

Just do it now;

let me bleed.

Do the killing.

Set me free.

My shattered memories.

Alone, no more.

A hopeless echo,

until I'm gone.

Killer, Love

He whispers softly.

He hugs her warmly.

He likes her hair.

He walks on air.

He shows his love.

Maybe, sort of.

He says a prayer,

before despair.

Burning Desire

You will be my escort

in a dance of death

and a song of love.

Killing me slowly.

First, from within,

till nothing remains

of me and my dreams.

Dandelions of Wishes

Wherever I go,
always strange faces.
Unknown, forgotten.

I don't know anyone.
No one knows me.
I can't remember you.

Even if I cut off all dandelions
just to get one wish,
you'll never come back.

Searching deep inside my heart,
emptiness.

Bloodstained Knife

I'll be the dream you never had.

I'll be the one you wanted.

Roses in hand, stained with blood.

All my life I've been haunted.

A knife full of lust.

A love starts to rust.

Wake me up.

Wake me from this nightmare.

Dark, my Past

Echoes of my past.

Fractured, they can't last.

Memories or dreams?

This is all it is.

Scattered in my mind.

Hazy, all in white.

Wounded is my heart.

Abandoned in the dark.

My Demons

I'll fight my demons myself.

I don't need anyone's help.

I'm old enough to know best.

I can clean up my own mess.

Don't make me listen to you.

Don't tell me what to do.

I'm not your slave anymore.

I have my wings, I can go.

Leave me alone.

I cannot see.

Leave me alone.

I cannot breathe.

I'll let it all go.

Won't follow your lead.

I'll be who I want.

Just let me live.

Fate's Desire

If fate exists,

she must hate me.

For I can't be

with the one I love.

Red string of fate

or destiny.

Our ties have been cut.

In this life

or the next,

this love

will never be.

Even when it shines,

even when it's dark,

everything remains

darker than my heart.

Bitter is the truth.

Hollow is the lie.

Memories of youth,

please just let me die.

Dying Heart

An oath broken,

forever unspoken.

Forged from blood

and pain and love.

Remains hidden,

always forbidden.

In endless lies

our love dies.

The Older We Become

The seasons will pass.

Your flowers will wither

and leaves will fall,

along with me.

I won't be the same.

I won't be beautiful

and you'll forget

my wrinkled face.

If you ever come,

I hope you'll remember me.

Where are You?

Upon the dawn of day,

it's time I realize

I'm all alone.

Without you.

Without your touch

and your warm embrace.

Safe Cage

I'm trapped in my cocoon.

I'll always stay here.

I wish I could escape from it.

Escape from myself,

and the feelings that keep me
enclosed.

Of all I could ask,

I hope this sadness will go away

or else I will sink

into an eternal numbness.

Never Enough

In rivers of hatred,

and oceans of lust,

I'll roam forever,

until I am dust.

For all I have wished for

will never be mine,

and all that I own,

just pieces in time.

Painting Smiles

If only I could paint

a smile on your face,

erase your tears

and all your pain.

If only I could wipe your sadness,

make it all go away.

Then, you would still be with me

and I'd be yours again.

Weight of the World

Have you seen me?

Have you felt as I did?

I'm small.

I'm weak.

How could I ever carry

the weight of the world?

It is all too much

for someone like me.

Maybe another,

stronger and bigger,

will carry it one day.

She was his all.

She was his Queen.

The light of dawn.

A jewel, a dream.

But he grew cold,

and he forgot.

Sorrow and pain,

he vowed to love.

She begged for mercy.

She fought for more.

And then, she fell

like all Queens fall.

Rex meus et amica mea,

in tuum altum thronum,

cum coronam magnam.

Salva me, o majestatis.

Serva me, o majestatis. *

* My King, and my love,
  in your high throne,
  with your great crown.
  Save me, oh Majesty.
  Save me, oh Majesty.

Circus Monster

They laugh at me.

They don't see me, they can't.

The stage is empty, I'm all alone.

They laugh, they scream, they hurt
me.

I wish they knew;

I'm not the monster of the circus.

The real monsters hide behind huge
curtains.

Our Song

The last rites.

A forgotten melody.

A last encore.

I'll sing for you.

I'll sing until my last breath.

Until you look my way.

Until you look at me.

Before time passes

and you forget me.

The Seeds They Planted

Anger and hatred;

they both are the same.

They're eating me

from within.

Is it that wrong?

Am I to blame?

They are the ones,

who planted the seeds.

And the seeds grew,

stronger and stronger.

Deep inside me,

till they consumed me.

He saw her naked
with all her scars.
His heart of hatred
broke into parts.

He wished for freedom
into her eyes,
but lost his wisdom
inside his mind.

He saw the world
turning to dust.
The terror, the pain,
the loss of trust.

Let it all burn,

till we belong.

Let the world perish,

till we go home.

The Pain They Caused

The lies that they told me,

I will not believe.

The dreams that they stole,

I will follow them.

The heart that they broke,

I will learn to live.

The voice that they muted,

I will scream aloud.

The poison that I prepared,

They will sleep forever.

Thousand Pieces

Put my pieces

back together.

Make me whole again.

So I can be me

forever,

and the pain will end.

Indecisive Heart

Am I a fool?

I cannot tell.

Am I in prison

or am I in hell?

What do you see

in that old well?

Could it be me

or is it her?

Isn't it clear

or you can't see?

The water's clarity

will not deceive.

After I lost you,

my world, a chaos.

I pray to gods,

to demons, to devils.

Someone, sometime,

will bring you back.

Resurrection, reincarnation.

I'll be with you again.

I'll find you once more.

Soon, my love.

Soon, with me.

Shattered

A beautiful mind,

damaged and kind.

All from the past,

should stay behind.

Broken pieces,

a test of time.

I'll put together

without a lie.

Fated to Meet You

The past has called.

Now, will you go?

Be someone else,

and let all go?

The girl from future

will bring back hope.

An ancient curse

must now be solved.

Fate, inevitable.

Death's cruel hands.

Robotic Heart

Betrayed.

Broken.

Hurt feelings

beautifully locked

inside an untrusting heart.

Just like a robot,

I'll stand my ground.

Never give up.

Never surrender.

I'll do what I must.

Inner Monsters

I won't lose.

I refuse to be defeated.

My enemies are close.

I will win,

but, even if I die,

a new day will rise.

A new tomorrow.

A dawn to a new life,

to a new me.

Eternity

I had a vision,

I had a dream.

Just a split second

of how our life could be.

If you could love me

the way I do...

If we could both

just start anew...

Till death I'll follow you,

till death us two.

Harmony

When the earth is dead,

and trees no longer breathe life.

When mountains crumble,

and volcanoes melt.

When ashes are your oxygen,

and rain is no longer cold.

When rivers, filled with blood,

cry on dried oceans.

Then, harmony will prevail,

and we'll belong to ourselves.

Cave of Dreams

Oh, cave of wonders,

What can you do?

I ask for honor,

for peace, for truth.

I want to dream.

I want to hope,

a great tomorrow

will come by dawn.

In colorful meadows,

I want to play,

lay on flowers,

wind in my hair.

Oh, cave of wonders,

have you not seen?

The death of man

is nearing in.

Midnight's Dance

Under the full moon's bright light,

they danced,

giving in to their feelings.

They prayed and prayed

for that moment to last forever.

Just a bit more...

Until our wings won't fly anymore.

One moment more.

Don't cry for me.

You'll find me on the darkest winter
night,

when all autumn leaves have fallen.

On the coldest summer day,

when all colors have faded from
flowers of spring.

I will be there.

There, for you.

Forever, with you.

When all is gone

and the world is ours.

Lullaby of Hope

A little piece of hope

I'll give to you tonight.

I'll give you all my love,

and I will hold you tight.

No harm will come your way,

as long as you're with me.

I'll never go away.

So, please don't forget me.

Eternal Wish

Open your wings now.

Carry me home.

There's nowhere else

I could go.

You are my dream now.

You are my hope.

A wish that I made

long ago.

Biography

Despoina Kemeridou was born in 1996 in Thessaloniki, Greece. She is studying Midwifery at the International University of Greece.

She has been into landscape photography since 2017. In her free time, she likes to draw. She started writing in 2009 and hence, understood that this is what she always wanted to do. Her first book, Fated to Meet You, was self-published in 2018. In 2020, she self-published her second book, Mark of a Demon. Currently, she's working on a dark short story

collection and an urban fantasy
novella.

Fated to Meet You

"I love you with every fiber of my being, Eleanor, but this love won't keep me alive, nor will it be able to protect you."

When Nora finds herself in the past, away from her mundane life, she chooses to take the place of a dead Princess. An arranged marriage with the soon-to-be King of the neighboring kingdom will help her discover love, friendship and hidden secrets.

An ancient curse has been haunting the royal family for ages. Will she be able to break it and save her loved ones from the cruel hands of death?

Time is already running out...

You can find it on Amazon

More From The Author

Mark of a Demon

"One day I will return — wait for me. I will return to take back what's mine."

When Heather was born, everyone thought she would die due to her weak heart. Upon her mother's callings, a demon showed up and saved her life by sharing his heart with hers. There was only one condition; she would live until the demon's powers ran out. Not knowing anything about the mark she had on her chest from the day she remembers herself, she falls in love with the demon, marking the start of a forbidden love...

What happens when she finds out the secrets her aunt and the demon have been keeping deeply hidden from her?

You can find it on Amazon